Garage
Maths

About Starters Maths books

STARTERS MATHS have been designed to highlight for young children some everyday situations, to which New Mathematics apply. The topic approach has been used to help the children relate mathematics to the ordinary world around them, by presenting money, number, shape, size and other mathematical ideas in familiar contexts. Children will be able to consolidate their experience in arranging sets, in recognising simple geometric forms and in using other mathematical ideas in ways now widely practised by their teachers. The books also follow the normal school practice of using only metric measures.

The text of each book is simple enough to enable children to read the questions for themselves, as the vocabulary has been carefully controlled to ensure that about 90% of the words used will be familiar to them.

Illustrated by: Joe Hall

Written and planned by: Leslie Foster, former Primary School Headmaster and Inspector for Schools, author of *Colour Factor in Action, Play's the Thing, Classes and Counts, Countdown to Christmas, Countdown to Easter* and *Just Look At Computers.*

Managing editor: Su Swallow

Editor: Sandie Oram

Production: Rosemary Bishop

Chairman, teacher panel: F. F. Blackwell, former General Inspector for Schools, London Borough of Croydon, with responsibility for Primary Education.

Teacher panel: Ruth Lucas, Linda Snowden, Mary Todd

ISBN 0 356 04429 7
(cased edition)

ISBN 0 356 11096 6
(limp edition)

© Macdonald and Company (Publishers) Limited 1973
Reprinted 1974 and 1984
Made and printed in Great Britain by Hazell, Watson & Viney Limited Aylesbury, Buckinghamshire

First published in 1973 by Macdonald and Company (Publishers) Limited
Maxwell House
Worship Street
London EC2A 2EN

Members of BPCC plc

STARTERS MATHS

Garage Maths

Macdonald Educational

There are many shapes in the garage.
Can you find some of them?
Do you see the shape of a cylinder?
Find a circle and a triangle.

2

These cans of oil are for sale.
Can you see the patterns they make?
Find different ways of arranging ten cans.
Make some patterns with ten dots.

3

This is a set of vehicles.
They are sorted into sub-sets.
How many are in each sub-set?
What could you put in the empty sub-set?

4

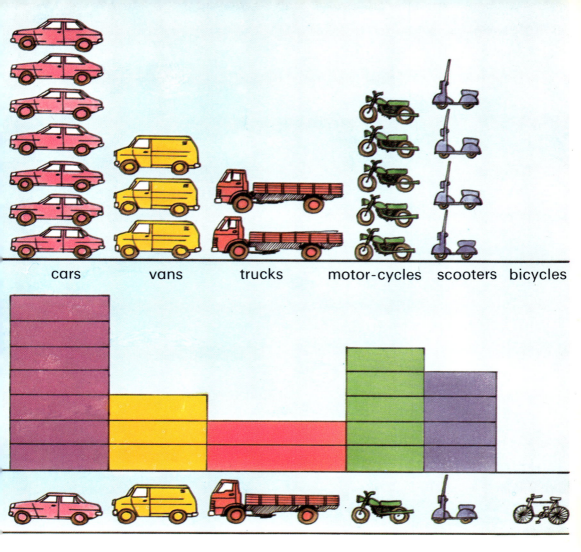

cars   vans   trucks   motor-cycles scooters bicycles

These graphs show the same vehicles.
The top one is in pictures.
The bottom one is a block graph.
Make graphs like this for your toys.

Petrol and oil are liquids.
Liquids are measured in litres.
How many litres of petrol were sold?
How many litres does each can hold?

6

The car has a tank for petrol.
The tanker is full of petrol.
It is filling the underground tank.
Which is the biggest tank?

These vehicles are being lifted.
How do we lift cars to change wheels?
How does the breakdown van lift a car?
Can you see the other ways of lifting?

These two cars have broken down.
How are they moved?
What other things do we move
by pushing and pulling?

9

Put the longest car
in the longest garage.
Put the other cars in their garages.

10

A

B

C

D

Copy these on paper.
Can you fill the boxes?
D is longer than C

[ ] is longer than [ ]

[ ] is longer than [ ]

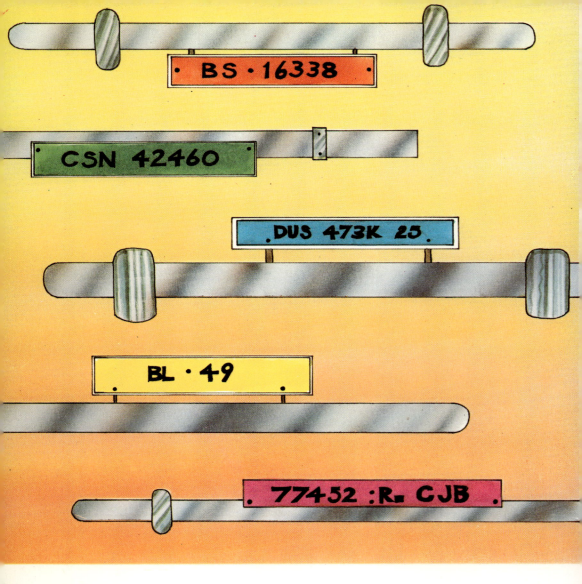

Here are some number plates.
How many fours can you see?
What numeral is shown most times?

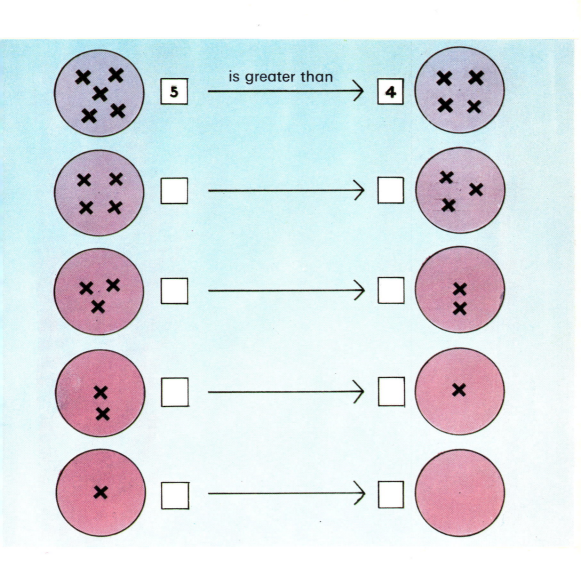

is greater than

5 → 4

Can you copy these and finish them?

These men are trying to move things.
Which way do you think is easiest?
14

These pictures show a wheel turning.
Which picture shows a $\frac{3}{4}$ turn?
What pattern does the wheel make?
Draw it with your fingers.

Count the trucks in the garage.
How many more cars are there than trucks?
Are there more vehicles or more trucks?

16

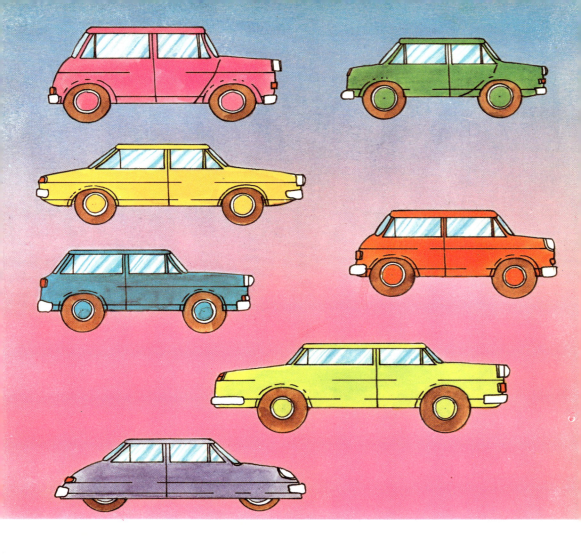

How many cars can you see?
If they faced the other way,
how many would there be?

Many things are measured in the garage.
So numbers are used a lot.
One dial shows the pressure of the tyre.
What does the other number show?

18

Each motorist wants 20 litres.
How many litres do the dials show?
How many more litres
does each motorist need?
15, 5 → 20

Men use force when they push a car.
Force is needed to turn
nuts with spanners
and to pull things out with pliers.

20

How does the boy stretch the spring?
Put a load on a spring balance.
Put a load on an elastic band.
What happens?

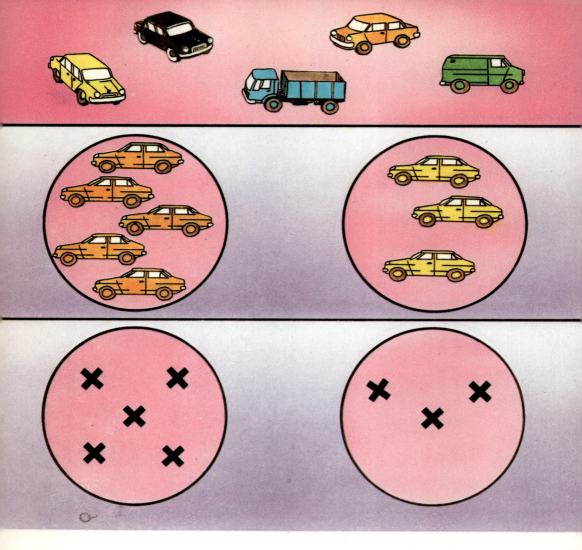

Can you make up some more like these?

5 is 2 more than 3

3 is 2 less than   5

2,3 ⟶ 5

22

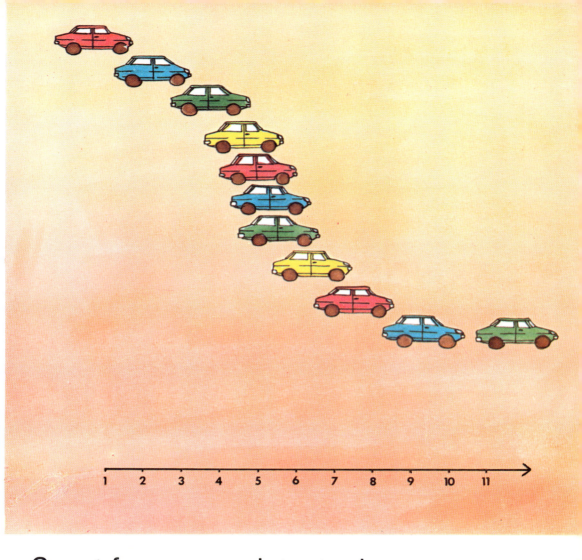

Count from one red car to the next.
How many did you count?
Start at 9 on the number line.
Where do you land if you count back 6?

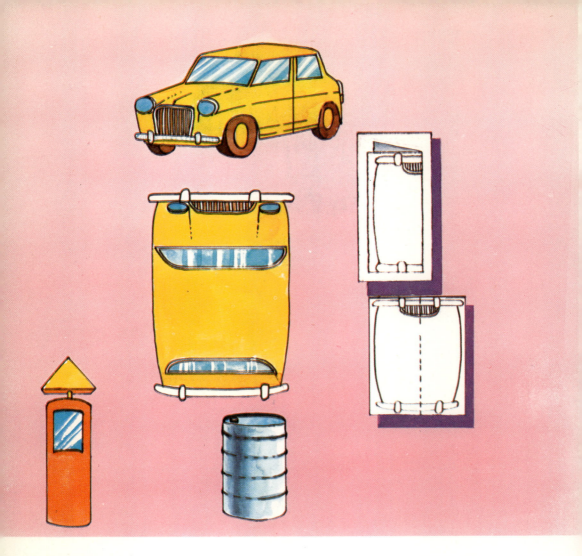

This car is the same on both sides.
This is called symmetry.
Fold some paper and tear out a shape.
Is the pattern symmetrical?

24

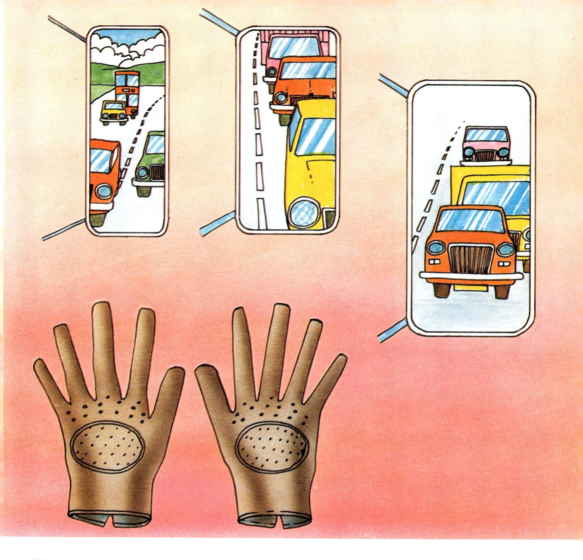

The mirror helps the driver
to see behind him.
The mirror reflects things.
Look at some reflections in a mirror.

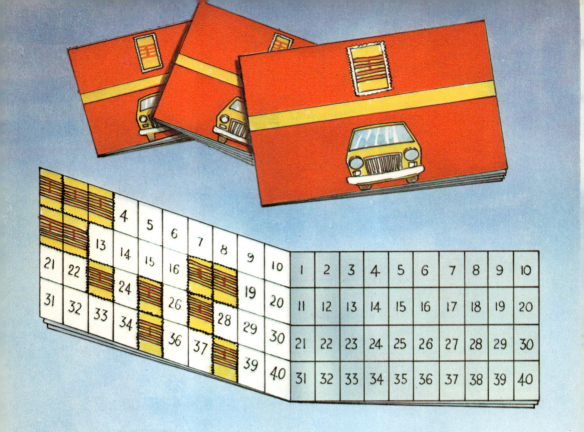

The driver is given some trading stamps.
He sticks them in a book.
How many more stamps does he need
to cover the left-hand page?

26

1	2	3	4	5	6	7	8	9	10
11	12	13	14	15	16	17	18	19	20
21	22	23	24	25	26	27	28	29	30
31	32	33	34	35	36	37	38	39	40

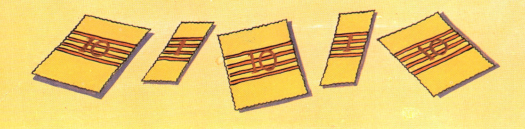

40 small stamps will fill the page.
This is worth the same as four 10 stamps.
Can you count in tens?

Index

cylinder
(page 2)

circle
(page 2)

triangle
(page 2)

vehicles
(page 4)

graph
(page 5)

wheel
(page 8)

dial
(page 18)

spanner
(page 20)

pliers
(page 20)

spring balance
(page 21)

symmetry
(page 24)

reflection
(page 25)

Notes for Parents and Teachers

Here is a brief explanation of the various mathematical points covered in this book, to help the interested adult to explore the topic with children.

Sets and numbers
(pages 2, 3, 10, 11, 12, 13, 16, 17, 22, 23)

Sets are one of the starting points of modern mathematics. Children sort things into sets and put them in order of size, colour or type *(3, 10)*. They also use sets in various opportunities for counting, with which they can develop an understanding of the processes involved in addition, subtraction and division *(11, 12, 13, 16, 17, 22)*. By arranging a number of objects into different patterns, they begin to understand that, though the arrangement may vary, the number remains constant *(4, 17)*.

Quantities
(pages 6, 7, 15, 18, 19)

Children learn the various terms used in general mathematical comparisons *(7, 18)* and the more specific terms of metric measures *(6, 19)*. They are also shown practical applications for simple fractions *(15)*.

Space
(pages 2, 15, 23, 24, 25, 26, 27)

Children learn about simple geometric shapes and discover their names *(2)*. They practise counting on number lines and in standard units *(23, 27)*. They begin to understand about rotation and area, helped by practical examples *(15, 26)*. Symmetry and reflection are also used to help them to understand more about shape *(24, 25)*.

Mechanisms
(pages 8, 9, 14, 20, 21)

Science and mathematics are closely linked studies. Simple mechanisms which illustrate force, such as pulleys, pushing and pulling activities, wheels and springs, are now included in most maths courses.

Pictorial representation
(page 5)

Pictorial representation by graphs of various kinds is one way for children to learn analysis, and it enables them to store information conveniently as well as to interpret it.